MARY G-
March 2014

THE SECRETS OF
IRELAND

METRO BOOKS
New York

An Imprint of Sterling Publishing
387 Park Avenue South
New York, NY 10016

Publisher and Creative Director: Nick Wells
Project Editor: Sara Robson
Art Director and Layout Design: Mike Spender
Digital Design and Production: Chris Herbert

Special thanks to: Helen Crust, Sarah Goulding, Polly Prior, Melinda Révèsz and Digby Smith

Kevin Eyres (author) qualified as an arts teacher at the UEA. He has a master's degree in European cultural policy. As well as writing extensively on modern art and media related topics, Kevin has written on various aspects of Irish cultural life and the great Irish literary figures of the nineteenth and twentieth centuries. One of his earliest memories is riding to the local creamery on a horse and cart to deliver milk from his grandparents' farm on the Kerry/Limerick borders.

Picture Credits
Courtesy of Corbis/The Irish Image Collection: 80, 174; The Irish Image Collection (www.theirishimagecollection.ie): 21, 22, 23, 35, 37, 40–41, 42, 43, 46, 50, 51, 52, 53, 55, 56, 57, 58, 59, 63, 68, 69, 70, 71, 72, 73, 76, 77, 78, 96, 97, 98, 99, 100–01, 102, 103, 105, 118, 119, 120–21, 122, 123, 124–25, 133, 135, 136, 150–51, 152, 155, 156–57, 188; iStock: 36; Shutterstock: 111; Vic, Mike and Paul Guy (www.vkguy.co.uk): 12, 13, 14–15, 16, 17, 18–19, 20, 24, 25, 26, 27, 28–29, 30, 31, 32, 33, 34, 38, 39, 44–45, 47, 54, 62, 64, 65, 66–67, 79, 81, 82–83, 84, 85, 86–87, 88, 89, 90–91, 92, 93, 104, 106–07, 108, 109, 110, 112–13, 114, 115, 126, 127, 128, 129, 130–31, 132, 134, 137, 138, 139, 140, 141, 144, 145, 146, 147, 148, 149, 153, 154, 160, 161, 162–63, 164, 165, 166–67, 168, 169, 170, 171, 172–73, 175, 176–77, 178, 179, 180, 181, 182–83, 184, 185, 186, 187, 189. All images from prelim pages and section dividers can all be found in the main body of the book and are credited above.

ISBN: 978-1-4351-3279-5

For information about custom editions, special sales, and premium and corporate purchases, please contact Sterling Special Sales at 800-805-5489 or specialsales@sterlingpublishing.com.

Manufactured in China

5 7 9 10 8 6 4

www.sterlingpublishing.com

THE SECRETS OF
IRELAND

Kevin Eyres

METRO BOOKS
NEW YORK

CONTENTS

INTRODUCTION

May the road rise to meet you.
May the wind be always at your back.
May the sun shine warm upon your face.
And rains fall soft upon your fields.
(Anon)

The secrets of Ireland are to be found in a land of great heroes and heroines, of myths and legends, monumental castles and elegant country houses, of gentle rain and lush green pastures, of towering cliffs, tranquil river estuaries and magnificent lakes. It is the land of Fionn MacCul (Finn MacCool) and Cúchulainn,

of James Joyce and Brendan Behan, of Jonathan Swift and W.B. Yeats, of George Bernard Shaw and Oscar Wilde.

Perhaps we should define what we mean by Ireland. The 32 counties that make up the third largest island in Europe are currently divided into the Republic of Ireland (Eire), and Northern Ireland: one of the four countries of the United Kingdom. The story that led to this division is, as we shall see, a long one and has shaped much of the country's turbulent history. However, the Ireland of this book is one land: the emerald isle that sits at Europe's most westerly point, forming a bulwark against the might of the Atlantic Ocean.

To appreciate the secrets of Ireland we have to know something of its history. Only by being aware of Ireland's past can we start to understand the importance of the enduring relationship that the people of Ireland have had with their country and how this has shaped, and continues to shape, both themselves and their island.

Ireland's modern history, which begins with the arrival of the Celts in 700 BC, has been one of turmoil, invasion, occupation and assimilation. As a small island divided into smaller, often-warring, kingdoms, Ireland was prey to opportunistic invaders, and almost continual internal conflict. Finally, with the arrival of St Patrick and Christianity in the fifth century, came three centuries of relative calm and prosperity. This golden age was itself ended by the arrival of increasingly large forces of marauding Vikings from AD 790 onwards.

The Vikings, lured by the wealth of the many Christian monasteries that flourished throughout the country, soon established themselves in Ireland and built fortified settlements at what are now Dublin, Waterford, Cork and Limerick. Following Brian Boru's decisive defeat of their forces in 1014, many Vikings remained, adopting the language, laws and culture of the native Celtic population.

This pattern of invasion and assimilation, rather than outright colonisation, continued with the arrival of the Anglo-Normans in 1169. In the fourteenth century, the English Crown sought to re-establish the division between the native Irish and the Anglo-Normans by introducing the draconian Statutes of Kilkenny. These laws attempted to prohibit the growth of the Irish language and culture, banning intermarriage and even forbidding native-born Irish from entering walled towns. In spite of these measures, the Anglo-Normans continued to adopt the indigenous Gaelic culture. The English Reformation of 1530, and the subsequent dissolution of the monasteries in 1536, changed everything.

Henry VIII's break with Rome, and the establishment of the Protestant Church in England, added a religious element to the political mix that was to reverberate down the centuries, and, even in the twenty-first century, has yet to be resolved. During the reigns of Elizabeth I and James I, the policy of Plantations was introduced. Lands and estates were confiscated from the native Catholic Irish and given to Protestant English (and later Scottish) immigrants. A brief period of Irish independence after the 1641 rebellion was followed by Cromwell's brutal re-assertion of English rule in 1652. These early dreams of home rule were finally crushed at the Battle of the Boyne in 1690.

Over the next century, the Protestant colonizers themselves became part of Irish society and began to lobby England for greater independence. More alarmingly for the English, a number of radical movements were springing up demanding greater rights for the downtrodden Catholic majority, including

the right to vote. Limited Catholic emancipation was finally achieved in 1829, but the cynical and uncaring reaction of the English and Anglo-Irish landlords to the suffering of the Catholic Irish during the terrible potato famines of 1845–49 led to much more widespread radical republicanism. At the same time, Gladstone's attempts to introduce Home Rule led the increasingly Protestant northeast of Ireland to organize and lobby against what they feared would be the loss of the political and economic advantages they had been granted by the English over the previous two centuries.

Events moved swiftly in the early part of the twentieth century. The Home Rule Act was passed in 1914, despite trenchant opposition from Ulster Protestants, only to be immediately suspended by the outbreak of the First World War. The 1916 Easter Uprising in Dublin, an abortive attempt to wrestle power from the English, was followed in 1919 by

finally defeating the anti-treaty Irish Republican Army (IRA). The implications of this tumultuous period – almost a century ago – are still being felt today. The Irish Republic's two main parties, Fianna Fáil and Fine Gael, are the direct descendants of the two factions that fought out that tragic conflict.

The Irish Free State finally became the Republic of Ireland in 1949 when it left the British Commonwealth. Today the six counties of Northern Ireland remain part of the United Kingdom. Northern Ireland's painful recent history is part of a sequence of events that stretches back to the Plantations of the sixteenth century and further back to the Anglo-Norman invasions of the twelfth century.

It can be easy to forget that behind the laid-back pace of life and the easy-going, hospitable nature of the Irish lies a turbulent, violent history. It is an enduring testament both to the Irish character and its culture that they have survived so harsh a history intact. As Sigmund Freud memorably remarked, 'This is one race of people for whom psychoanalysis is of no use whatsoever'.

Ireland's resolute struggle to maintain its own Gaelic culture in the face of successive waves of invaders has left a rich legacy not only in its monuments but also in its literature and its music. You can see this most clearly in the Irish-speaking Gaeltacht regions of the western counties, but throughout Ireland you will never be far away from powerful reminders of the genuine connection that the Irish feel for their rich oral and musical traditions.

Although Eire is nowadays a thriving and influential member of the European Union, with a booming economy and the sobriquet 'Celtic Tiger', it is still a largely rural nation. Northern Ireland is also flourishing and, though traditionally more industrialized than the Republic, it is also for the most part rural.

the unilateral declaration of an Irish Republic containing all the 32 counties. This led to another brutal Anglo-Irish war that culminated in the Anglo-Irish Treaty of 1921. The treaty was a compromise that replaced the Irish Republic with an Irish Free State, but allowed the six counties of Northern Ireland the option of opting out, which they immediately did.

At this point the Irish were fatally split between those who thought the Treaty too much of a compromise, and those who thought the deal was the best they could achieve at the time. A bloody and bitter civil war ensued with the pro-treaty faction

The Industrial Revolution, which caused so much upheaval in nineteenth-century England, did have an impact on the area around Belfast but bypassed the rest of Ireland almost entirely, leaving it largely unspoilt by urban blight and industrial decay even today.

The physical landscape of Ireland is a combination of the wild and rugged and the pastoral. In essence the topography is one of a dramatic coastline surrounding a less spectacular, albeit lushly beautiful, central plain. However, Ireland certainly manages to contain a remarkable variety of terrain within its relatively small area, from the towering cliffs of Slieve League in Donegal, to the rich pastures and raised bogs of Roscommon, and the serene lakes of Fermanagh. The 32 counties of Ireland offer a variety of unforgettable scenery that provides a fitting backdrop for the turmoil of its history, the wealth of its historic monuments and the warm, civilized nature of its people.

Ireland is traditionally divided into four provinces, historically referred to as kingdoms – Ulster, Connacht, Leinster, and Munster. A fifth province, Meath, now forms part of Leinster. To make your journey through *The Secrets of Ireland* easier to navigate, we have divided each of the four provinces into north and south regions.

As you explore the wonderfully evocative images that follow, remember that the beauty of Ireland is not the twee attractiveness of picture-postcard clichés, but the product of the visceral and often painful history of a proud and cultured people, and of their enduring love for their beautiful island.

ULSTER NORTH

Although today most people associate Ulster solely with Northern Ireland, ours is the Ulster of the four Kingdoms of Ireland and so includes three counties from Northern Ireland and one, Donegal, from the Republic.

If the reporting of the Troubles has shaped your impressions of Northern Ireland, you risk ignoring one of the most beautiful regions in the whole of Europe. The north coast can vie with anywhere in Ireland for breathtaking scenery. In County Down, where St Patrick first landed and where he lies buried, the Mountains of Mourne really do 'sweep down to the sea' revealing a coastline of golden beaches and picturesque fishing villages.

All the quiet beauty of County Antrim with its fertile green glens and wonderfully preserved Norman castles is overshadowed by the sheer spectacle of the Giant's Causeway, one of the great natural wonders of the world.

As the green fields and pastures of Londonderry merge into the wild mountains and rugged coastline of Donegal, the scenery changes again. Bearing the full brunt of the Atlantic, the towering cliffs of Slieve League are among the highest and most dramatic in Europe.

The north of Ulster is a wonderful introduction to the variety of riches that Ireland has to offer.

THATCHED SHOP
near Killybegs, Donegal

Sheltered from the worst of the Atlantic gales that batter nearby Slieve League, Killybegs is one of Ireland's principle fishing ports. Situated in a natural harbour, in summer it attracts thousands of anglers and tourists to its annual sea angling festival. Characteristic of Ireland's generally rather laid-back approach to the commercial opportunities of tourism is this thatched cottage, typical of those to be found throughout Donegal. With its whitewashed walls and casual air, who could resist stepping inside to find out more?

FOLK MUSEUM
Glencolumbkille, Donegal

Glencolumbkille, named after Saint Columba, is in the middle of the Gaeltacht (Irish speaking) region of south Donegal. Situated by a fine sandy beach at the end of a lushly fertile glen, this delightfully understated folk museum is set in a group of small farmhouses and barns. Among its exhibits is a replica of a National School and, more intriguingly, a sheebeen where locally brewed and untaxed liquor was sold away from the attention of the Revenue men.

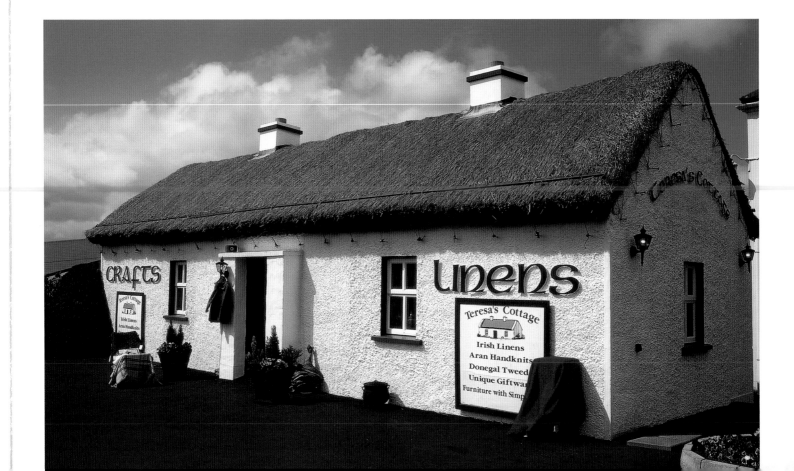

PORTSALON

Fanad Peninsula, Donegal

The north coast of Donegal has two great sea loughs, Lough Foyle and Lough Swilly. The Fanad Peninsula forms the western shore of Lough Swilly and its cliff-edge lighthouse bears testimony to the dangers of the wild coast and the power of the Atlantic. Portsalon, a sheltered spot at the mouth of the lough, was once a thriving seaside resort. Sadly it has lost its allure for holidaymakers, but its wonderful golden strand remains facing east towards the Inishowen Peninsula and Malin Head.

FANAD PENINSULA
near Rathmullan, Donegal

Further inland on the Fanad Peninsula, away from the rugged coastline, the countryside has a more pastoral air. Cows graze in green pastures in the shadow of gentle hills, while white clouds scud across the blue sky. Rathmullen itself is a pretty little seaside town, its houses tracing the gentle arc of the bay. Nearby is Rathmelton, an elegant Plantation town, founded in the seventeenth century as a base for incoming English colonizers.

MULROY BAY
Fanad Peninsula, Donegal

Under clear blue skies a yacht sits calmly at anchor in the unruffled waters of Mulroy Bay, an outstandingly beautiful marine inlet between the Fanad and Rosguill Peninsulas on Donegal's north coast. Although the inlet is little more than 350 m (1,155 ft) wide in places, driving between the two shores at the coast involves a journey of some 50 km (31 miles). For this reason, Mulroy Bay is soon to be spanned by a landmark bridge with a clearance height of 20 m (66 ft).

ATLANTIC DRIVE
Rosguill Peninsula, Donegal

Soft waves break on the evocatively named Atlantic Drive, a charming stretch of coast forming part of the west coast of the Rosguill Peninsula. The Drive is the continuation of the main street and beach of Downings, a lively resort on the headland of the peninsula. Looking north, Mulroy Bay is clearly visible with the hills of Inishowen in the distance. Looking at this summer scene it is hard to imagine how bleak and storm-tossed the winter months can be.

LURGYVALE COTTAGE
Kilmacrennan, Donegal

Who could resist a place called Lurgyvale Cottage? Just a little outside the inland village of Kilmacrennan is this delightful group of buildings clustered around a 150-year-old thatched cottage. As its name suggests, the cottage is situated on the wooded banks of the River Lurgy behind thickets of wild rhododendrons. The buildings have all been restored to their original state with open hearths and flagstone floors, and are now home to a traditional crafts and music centre.

SLIEVE LEAGUE
Donegal

The spectacular cliffs of Slieve League (the 'grey mountain') are the highest in Europe, rising precipitously from the turbulent waters of the Atlantic. But it isn't only their height that makes Slieve League such a dramatic site: the mighty cliff-faces constantly change hue, reflecting the weather around them. This is especially noticeable in the early morning and evening when the rising and setting of the sun produce giant splashes of amber and red across the imperious rock-faces.

RECONCILIATION MONUMENT
Londonderry City, Londonderry

Craigavon Bridge crosses the River Foyle, connecting
Londonderry's mainly Catholic Cityside with the predominantly
Protestant Waterside. At the end of the bridge, a bronze statue rises
optimistically above the traffic. Maurice Harron's sculpture *Hands
Across the Divide* shows two young men standing on separate raised
stone platforms, reaching out so that their fingertips can just touch
across the gap. It signifies the genuine desire to bridge the divide
that has existed in this part of Ireland for many hundreds of years.

GUILDHALL IN THE SNOW
Londonderry City, Londonderry

Londonderry's Guildhall stands resplendent in the winter
snow. Standing just outside the massive city walls, the Guildhall's
neo-Gothic elegance is a tribute to the wealth and influence of
Londonderry in the late nineteenth century when the Guildhall
was built. It survived being damaged by a serious fire in 1908
and being bombed in 1972, and has now been restored to its
original glory, acting as a civic and cultural centre for the
people of the city.

MUSSENDEN TEMPLE
Londonderry

The flamboyant eighteenth-century Earl of Bristol, Frederick Hervey, created an estate at Downhill not far from Castlerock to the north of Londonderry. Hervey spent a fortune on the house and gardens, erecting a series of neo-classical buildings in the grounds including the windswept Mussenden Temple, perched precariously on the clifftops. The temple was modelled on the Temple of Vesta at Tivoli near Rome and was originally designed as a library, though some say its real purpose was as a discreet rendezvous for romantic assignations.

PORTSTEWART STRAND
Londonderry

The elegant little town of Portstewart with its sheltered harbour was a popular resort with well-heeled Victorians. The town is named after the Scottish Stewart clan who built the town's first house. Such were the pretensions of the locals that the railway station was deliberately built a mile out of the town, to discourage the presence of riff-raff. From the town runs a series of impressive cliff walks overlooking the magnificent three-mile long Portstewart strand, now under the protection of the National Trust.

WHITE ROCKS
near Portrush, Antrim

Just along the coast, in County Antrim, is Portstewart's somewhat brasher neighbour, Portrush. Situated on Ramore Head, Portrush is a lively resort, not afraid to let its hair down. It has a world-class links (seaside) golf course and, like Portstewart, a splendid beach. Walk along the strand and you will be rewarded at the end of your promenade with the impressive site of White Rocks. These limestone cliffs have been fashioned into arches and caves by the relentless force of the wind and waves.

DUNLUCE CASTLE
Antrim

Built in the thirteenth century by Richard de Burgh, Earl of Ulster, the roofless ruins of Dunluce Castle stand imperious on the edge of a 30 m (100 ft) basalt cliff. The various local warring clans coveted control of such a strategically sited castle. In 1584, the MacDonnells captured the castle and used booty from a Spanish Armada fleet treasure ship – which ran aground nearby – to modernize it. However, when subsidence tipped the kitchens into the sea during a dinner in 1639, the castle was abandoned.

GIANT'S CAUSEWAY
Antrim

It is easy to see why our ancestors thought that the forty thousand regular, mostly hexagonal, basalt columns that make up the Giant's Causeway were more likely to be the work of mythical characters than the volcanic action that actually formed them. According to one legend, the great Irish hero Fionn MacCul (Finn MacCool) built the causeway to bring his love, a female giant who lived on the Hebredian island of Staffa, to his home in Ulster.

DUNSEVERICK CASTLE
Antrim

Little more than a ruined tower on a grassy promontory is all
that survives of historic Dunseverick Castle. The original castle,
built in 1525 BC, was the capital of the ancient Celtic kingdom
of Dal Raida, and was directly linked by royal road to Tara, the
mythical seat of the High Kings of Ireland. The ruins we see
here are part of a later castle built by the MacDonnell clan in
the sixteenth century and destroyed by Scottish forces in 1641.

WHITE PARK BAY
Antrim

Of all the wonderful golden beaches on the north coast of
Ulster, White Park Bay is one of its most admired. Overlooked
by Dunseverick Castle and surrounded by cliffs where wild
flowers thrive in spring and summer, the gentle sweep of the
bay disguises strong currents and dangerous tides. The perils
of bathing here have led to this lovely spot being largely
ignored by tourists. As a result the bay can only be accessed
on foot and has just one small car park.

BALLINTOY HARBOUR
Antrim

Around the next bay, a twisting narrow road leads down to a charming little harbour set into the limestone cliffs at Ballintoy. Overlooked by Sheep Island, which can just be seen in the distance across Boheeshane Bay, Ballintoy has been a popular refuge for coastal sailors and fishermen since the Iron Age and evidence exists of earlier occupation during the Neolithic period. A former landlord of Ballintoy, Dawson Downing was related to Sir George Downing after whom Downing Street in London is named.

CARRICK-A-REDE
Antrim

Those emboldened by a trip to the Giant's Causeway may want to test their heroic potential by walking across the rope bridge at nearby Carrick-a-Rede. This rather rudimentary structure is the only land access to a salmon fishery located on the tiny island just offshore. The twisting, flexing bridge spans some 20 m (66 ft) and hangs 25 m (83 ft) above the water. Crossing over to the island and back is a daunting prospect even allowing for the safety nets and robust handrails.

GLENS OF ANTRIM
Antrim

Over thousands of years, nine rivers carved the deep valleys
that form the Nine Glens of Antrim. In the eighteenth century,
this Gaelic speaking area was so wild and remote that the
Plantations didn't touch it. Today, each of the glens has its
own distinct character, from the Alpine charm of Glengariff
to the wildness of Glendun. The 'capital' of the Nine Glens
is the delightful village of Cushendall, where three glens meet
on their way to the sea.

THE WATERFRONT HALL
Belfast, Antrim

On the banks of the River Langan, in the elegant heart
of the city, is one of the most visible signs of the renaissance
of Belfast as a European city: the Waterfront Concert Hall.
Built at a cost of £32m and completed in just 39 months,
the Hall was opened in 1997. With its striking copper-domed
roof, designed to 'weather' and eventually match the dome of
Belfast's City Hall, the Waterfront Hall has become a striking
feature on the rapidly developing Belfast skyline.

STORMONT CASTLE
Belfast, Antrim

The imposing Portland stone and Mourne granite mass of Stormont was built as a symbol of the power and legitimacy of the newly established Northern Irish Parliament. Following Partition in 1921, Northern Ireland's legislative body originally met in the City Hall, finally moving in 1932 to their new home set in parklands some five miles outside the city of Belfast. The original plan for a building, similar to the Congress building in Washington, DC, was scrapped in favour of Sir Arnold Thornley's neo-classic design.

ORMEAU PARK
Belfast, Antrim

Snow-covered gates mark the entrance to Ormeau Park, an elegant riverside green space in the heart of Belfast. The estate, originally the home of the Marquis of Donegal, was sold to the City of Belfast to clear family debts and opened in 1871 as Belfast's first public park. Today it is the largest of the city's parks and marks the finish point for the Belfast marathon. Ormeau Park is one of three sites competing for the proposed City of Belfast stadium.

BALLYCOPELAND WINDMILL
near Millisle, Down

County Down has traditionally been a major centre for grain growing in Ireland, and windmills have been a feature of the landscape here since the eighteenth century. At one point there were over 100 working windmills in the county, though today only a few remain. The Ballycopeland Windmill, a mile west of the seaside resort of Millisle, is the only fully working mill to survive, having been restored to its original condition by the state as a heritage site.

SCRABO TOWER
near Newtownards, Down

Stately Scrabo Tower stands sentinel over Scrabo County Park. It was built in the 1850s as a memorial to Charles Stewart, third Marquis of Londonderry, who worked to help the victims of Ireland's terrible potato famine. The tower overlooks woodlands and disused quarries, where Scrabo stone was dug out and used locally as a building material. Greyabbey Monastery and Belfast's Albert Clock were both built using it, and in the early nineteenth century Scrabo stone was shipped to Dublin and even as far as New York.

MOUNT STEWART HOUSE
near Newtownards, Down

Although Mount Stewart House, on the east shore of Lough Strangford, is a fascinating building in its own right, it is the magnificent gardens surrounding the house that have made Mount Stewart internationally famous. Home to the Earls of Londonderry since the eighteenth century, the grounds were laid out in the 1920s by Edith, Lady Londonderry, the wife of the seventh marquis. Today, the 40 hectares (98 acres) of gardens are recognized as a World Heritage Site.

HILLSBOROUGH CASTLE
Down

Elegant Hillsborough Castle, originally built in 1650 by Colonel Arthur Hill to maintain control of the strategic Dublin to Carrickfergus road, now plays an important role in relations between Northern Ireland and the mainland. As well as being the official residence of the Queen when she is in the province, it is also the official residence of the Secretary of State for Northern Ireland. On the international stage, Hillsborough is best known as the place where the historic 1985 Anglo-Irish Agreement was signed.

WATERFALL
Crawfordsburn Country Park, Down

This attractive waterfall stands at the head of the glen in Crawfordsburn County Park, a delightful estate running along over two miles of Down's rugged coastline. As well as the waterfall, the park includes woodland, meadows, an elegant railway viaduct and a little village of whitewashed houses. Remarkably for an estate that was originally gifted to Scottish Presbyterians, it also contains the aptly named Old Inn that dates from 1614 and is said to be the oldest in Ireland.

MOURNE MOUNTAINS
Down

Of all the songs and laments written by homesick Irish emigrants far from home, it is 'The Mountains of Mourne' that remains the best known and closest to many Irish hearts. Percy French, a Roscommon man, composed the song in 1896 in collaboration with his musical partner, Houston Collisson. Before becoming a professional musician and performer, French had been an engineer and for seven years had the somewhat less glamorous occupation of County Cavan's Inspector of Drains.

THE SILENT VALLEY AND BEN CROM
Mourne Mountains, Down

Although the calm stillness of the Silent Valley and Ben Crom
seems almost pre-historic, these two lakes in the heart of the
Mourne Mountains bear the imprint of very recent human
intervention. In the early twentieth century, a dam and huge
reservoir were built in the Silent Valley to serve the growing
need of Belfast and the rest of County Down for fresh water.
In 1957 a further dam and artificial lake were constructed
nearby at Ben Crom.

NEWCASTLE
Down

Newcastle is the largest of County Down's many seaside resorts,
spreading along the north coast of Dundrum Bay. It was on the
bay's fine sandy beaches that Brunel's *Great Britain* was wrecked
in 1846, later to be salvaged and restored. Behind the town rises
the impressive bulk of Slieve Donard, which at 850 m (2,800 ft)
is Ulster's highest peak. But for many visitors it is the Royal,
County Down, a links golf course with a world-class reputation,
which makes Newcastle such an attractive spot.

ULSTER SOUTH

Ulster's four southern counties, though not as dramatic as those of the north, have a tranquil rural charm that repays closer inspection. This is a country of quiet back roads, imposing lakes and rivers, forests, and gentle mountains.

Cavan's boast of a lake for every day of the year may be a little exaggerated, but its labyrinthine network of lakes and rivers provide a unique setting for gentle hills and small islands. Armagh and Tyrone border onto Lough Neagh, the largest lake in the United Kingdom, while the majestic River Erne flows gently through Fermanagh forming Upper and Lower Lough Erne, whose many inlets and islands provide a welcome sanctuary for a great variety of birds.

The south of Ulster also has its share of historic sights. Monaghan's Bronze Age settlements and pre-historic remains, Fermanagh's island monasteries and Eamhain Macha (Navan Fort), the ceremonial capital of the ancient kingdom of Ulster, are significant parts of Ireland's heritage.

The understated and easy-going atmosphere of the south of Ulster is perfectly captured in the Georgian elegance of Armagh City, home to the remains of the High King of Ireland Brian Boru who, in 1014, finally defeated the Viking invaders at the bloody Battle of Clontarf.

BALLYKEEL DOLMEN
Armagh

Standing alone by the roadside is the Ballykeel Dolmen, known by locals as the Hag's Chair. Ballykeel Dolmen is a megalith, a Neolithic tomb built with large stones and originally enclosed in a mound of earth. There are four types of megalith and Ballykeel is an outstanding example of a portal tomb, comprising three large upright stones supporting a capstone. Two larger stones form the entrance to the tomb while a third, smaller one, balances the sloping 'roof' stone.

ST PATRICK'S CATHEDRAL
Armagh City, Armagh

There are two cathedrals in Armagh City, the place where St Patrick, the first bishop of Armagh, built Ireland's first cathedral in AD 445. St Patrick's Church of Ireland Cathedral is built on the site of St Patrick's original church, and is a much restored and revised medieval structure. St Patrick's Catholic Cathedral, pictured here, dates from the middle of the nineteenth century and has been described as a triumph of the neo-Gothic style, with its twin towers and soaring mosaic-clad interior.

BEAGHMORE STONE CIRCLES

near Cookstown, Tyrone

Situated in a remote corner of County Tyrone, the Beaghmore Stone Circles are a truly remarkable collection of standing stones. Although the individual stones are not especially large, their number and complexity make this an important Bronze Age site. The site comprises seven circles, ten stone rows and a number of burial mounds. Some of the stone formations were used for astronomical observations and others for ceremonial purposes. Even on a bright summer's day, a tangible air of mystery permeates this ancient monument.

ULSTER HISTORY PARK

near Omagh, Tyrone

In 1985, work began on the site of the Ulster History Park and five years later the 14-hectare (35-acre) site was officially opened. Set in the foothills of the beautiful Sperrin Mountains, the Park gives an impression of life in Ulster from the earliest Stone Age settlements onwards. By meticulously following original building methods and avoiding the worst excesses of modern theme park attractions, the History Park gives an authentic introduction to the rich social history of the region.

SPERRIN MOUNTAINS
Tyrone

Although not the most immediately dramatic of mountain ranges, the Sperrins are a much-loved, if sparsely populated, region. Wild, and with a desolate beauty all of their own, they are an unforgettable sight in spring and summer when the undulating hills are a mass of vivid yellow gorse. Although few people live in the Sperrins, the area is alive with all kinds of wildlife, including buzzards and hawks that circle silently in wait of unsuspecting prey.

ENNISKILLEN CASTLE
Fermanagh

Strikingly floodlit, the vast Portland stone flank and Watergate tower of Enniskillen Castle are reflected in the still waters of the River Erne. The castle was originally built in the fifteenth century by the Maguire clan but was leased to Sir William Cole, an Englishman, during the Plantations of the seventeenth century. A series of repairs, refurbishments and additions over the years, reflecting its strategic importance to the English Crown, led to it becoming a barracks for the Royal Inniskilling Fusiliers.

DEVENISH ISLAND
Lower Lough Erne, Fermanagh

Lough Erne's network of islands was home to many monastic
and church communities in the Middle Ages. The most
significant of these settlements was founded on Devenish
Island in the sixth century. Although it was raided and finally
burned by Vikings, it later flourished, becoming the site of
a fine Romanesque church, now destroyed. An Augustinian
Priory and an exceptionally well preserved twelfth century
round tower remain. The evocative ruins and the island setting
make this a wonderfully tranquil place.

HILTON PARK
Monaghan

The original house at Hilton Park was built in the seventeenth
century, and when the Madden family bought the estate in
1734, they started a programme of alterations and improvements
to both the house and the grounds. Undeterred by a serious
fire in 1803, the Maddens continued transforming the estate
throughout the nineteenth century. The current owner,
Johnny Madden, who is the eighth generation of Maddens
at Hilton Park, has restored the house and its grounds to
their Victorian splendour.

CROMWELL'S BRIDGE
River Cabra, Dun An Rí, Cavan

The Dun an Rí Forest Park in County Cavan, though small, has more than its share of history and legend. The 'Romantic Glen' of the Cabra River, which flows through the park, is said to have been where the great Irish hero Culchulain camped during his campaign against the forces of Queen Maeve. Further along the river is Cromwell's Bridge, which Oliver Cromwell and his army are believed to have crossed on their march to confront the O'Reilly clan at Muff Castle.

TRADITIONAL PUB
Cartlans, Kingscourt, Cavan

No Irish village would be complete without its pub, no matter how small. The public house has played a central role in Irish social history ever since it began to emerge in the Middle Ages as a place where travellers could find refreshment, and possibly buy provisions. Village pubs in Ireland traditionally played this dual role as the local shop, or they were simply houses where people gathered to drink and talk. Cartlans' delightful thatched pub in Kingscourt looks like just such a place.

CONNACHT NORTH

The province of Connacht contains some of Ireland's most wonderful treasures. It also bears the marks of the suffering of its people, especially during the two great Irish famines of the eighteenth and nineteenth centuries.

There is a remote starkness to much of the landscape here that sits well with the traditional way of life of its Irish-speaking Gaeltacht areas. From the fine mountains, lakes and beaches of Leitrim and Sligo that inspired Ireland's greatest poet, W.B. Yeats, to the wild and breathtaking landscapes of Mayo and Clare Island, the north of Connacht transports us back to an earlier Ireland. Much of the area is still relatively primitive and retains the spirit of Gaelic Ireland perhaps better than anywhere else in the country. It is typical of the pace of life in Connacht that the first traffic lights in County Leitrim were not installed until 2003.

The influence of the Catholic Church can be felt especially strongly here. Every year, thousands of pilgrims follow in the footsteps of St Patrick climbing the holy mountain of Croagh Patrick, often barefoot. Further inland, the apparition of the Virgin Mary in 1879 has led to the small town of Knock becoming an internationally important Catholic shrine.

DOO LOUGH PASS
Mayo

The sombre Doo Lough Pass near the wild west coast of County Mayo runs between the Mweelrea Mountains and the Sheeffry Hills, close to the border with County Galway. At the head of this beautiful valley is a poignant monument commemorating a tragic incident that took place during the Great Famine. When in 1849, 600 starving locals marched through the pass to nearby Delphi to ask their English landlord for food, he refused their pleas and over 400 died on their journey home.

CLEW BAY AND CROAGH PATRICK
Mayo

The mountain known as Croagh Patrick towers above Clew Bay on the western coast of Mayo, which contains excellent examples of sunken drumlins, elongated glacial hills and many tiny islands. St Patrick, the patron saint of Ireland, is said to have fasted for 40 days and nights on the mountain. During this time, he banished the large colonies of birds that lived there because they contained the demons of paganism and were trying to distract him from his fast. He instead invited angelic birds that soothed him with their songs.

AASLEAGH FALLS
near Leenane, Mayo

The village of Aasleagh is situated at the mouth of the River Erriff as it runs into Killary Harbour, Ireland's only fjord. Just above the village, the waters of the Erriff tumble over the rocks of the picturesque Aasleagh Falls on their way to the sea. The Erriff is one of the premier salmon fishing rivers in Ireland and fly-fisherman travel here from all over the world to test their skills on the river's eight miles of prime angling water.

ACHILL BEG ISLAND
Mayo

Just off the southern coast of Achill Island is tiny Achill Beg Island. Today a few holiday homes are the only signs of habitation, but the island sustained a small community in the centre of the island until 1965, and the signs of agriculture can still be seen on the hilly slope running down the shore. In the same year that the last resident left, a lighthouse was established on the island to coincide with the closure of the light on nearby Clare Island.

CLARE ISLAND
Mayo

Standing guard over the entrance to Clew Bay is the striking silhouette of Clare Island, seen here as we look south from Achill Island. Clare is the largest of the multitude of islands in the bay and has supported a sizeable community for the last 5,000 years. In the sixteenth century, Clare Island was the stronghold of the pirate queen Grace O'Malley, who lies buried in the tiny thirteenth century Cistercian Abbey at Abbeyknockmoy. The abbey is internationally famous for its fine medieval wall paintings.

CLASSIEBAWN CASTLE
Mullaghmore, Sligo

The building of Classiebawn Castle, high on Mullaghmore Head, was begun by Lord Palmerston, then Prime Minister of England, and completed by his son in 1874. The construction was a major undertaking, as the castle was built entirely of Donegal stone brought by sea to the site. Palmerston also had a harbour created below the house, and it was from here in 1979 that Lord Mountbatten tragically sailed to his death on board his yacht *Shadow V*, blown up by the IRA.

MONASTIC RUINS
Inishmurray Island, Sligo

North along the coast past Sligo Bay lies the uninhabited island of Inishmurray, five miles off the mainland and fully exposed to the might of the Atlantic. In spite of its inhospitable location the island managed to support a small community of farmers and fishermen until 1948, when the end of the ferry service and closing of the island school forced the last inhabitants to leave for the mainland. Little remains today but the extensive ruins of the sixth century abbey of Saint Molaise.

BEN BULBEN
Sligo

The flat-topped profile of 'bare Ben Bulben' rises spectacularly from Sligo's coastal plain to its 520 m (1,715 ft) summit overlooking Donegal Bay. This magical limestone massif, seen here from the Donegal side, changes shape dramatically as you round it. Irish mythology tells how Fionn MacCul (Finn MacCool), after searching for seven years, found his son Oisin wandering naked on the mountainside. In the graveyard of the somewhat austere church at Drumcliff, under the shadow of the mountain, Ireland's great poet William Butler Yeats lies buried.

MARKREE CASTLE
Collooney, Sligo

The Cooper family, who currently own Markree Castle, were originally gifted the estate by Oliver Cromwell in lieu of wages owed to Edward Cooper, a young officer in Cromwell's invading English army. Edward married the widow of the leader of the defeated O'Brien clan and settled down to life in County Sligo. Today Charles Cooper, a direct descendent of Edward's third son, owns the castle, which he has run as a hotel since 1989.

PARKES CASTLE
Lough Gill, Leitrim

Parkes Castle's idyllic location on the banks of Lough Gill overlooks the lake isle of Innisfree, immortalized by W.B. Yeats' poem of the same name. This attractive Plantation castle was built in the early seventeenth century by Robert Parker on the site of an earlier fortress, which he demolished to provide the stones for the new building. The castle has recently been extensively restored and today looks much as it did when Parker took up residence in 1610.

GLENCAR WATERFALL
Leitrim

Although Glencar is not the most spectacular of waterfalls, there is something enchanting about the way the water cascades into the lake. Like so many of County Sligo and County Leitrim's beauty spots, Glencar Waterfall, just a short distance south of Manorhamilton, was the inspiration for one of W.B. Yeats' poems, 'The Stolen Child'. Like much of Yeats' work, it expresses nostalgia for what he considered the more romantic, innocent Ireland of the past.

CONNACHT SOUTH

Galway and Roscommon are a good example of the abrupt contrast between the landscapes around the coasts and those of the inland areas of Ireland.

West Galway and the Aran Islands, with their gaily-painted cottages, are some of Ireland's most austerely beautiful areas. The influence of the country's past and its proud Gaelic heritage are apparent everywhere in this sparsely populated region. Travel inland through the Connemara Mountains from the ragged coast where they rise dramatically from the sea, to the shores of Lough Conn and Lough Corrib, and you find yourself in a land far removed from the turmoil of the twenty-first century.

By contrast, Galway City is one of the fastest-growing metropolitan areas in Europe. It maintains its position at the heart of Gaelic culture, while vigorously pursuing a policy of expansion. Galway is reaching out to be recognized as a modern city of culture, and is already famous for its international arts festivals and the quality of its hospitality.

County Galway, east of Lough Corrib and Roscommon, is far more pastoral. This lowland region of Connacht is an area of rich grazing land, extensive peat bogs and fertile farmland.

BOYLE ABBEY
Roscommon

The Cistercian order of monks founded Boyle Abbey in 1161 as a sister abbey for Mellifont, their first abbey in Ireland, which they established twenty years earlier. In common with all Cistercian abbeys, Boyle was constructed according to the plan of St Gall and consists of a group of structures that form a square arranged around a central lawned area. The abbey was converted into a fortified castle by Cromwell's English forces in 1659, but survives today remarkably intact.

CASTLE ISLAND
Lough Key Forest Park, Boyle, Roscommon

Lough Key, often described as Ireland's loveliest stretch of inland water, is a five km- (three mile-) wide circular lake in the heart of the Lough Key Forest Park. Castle Island is one of the lake's 33 islands and the site of a ruined nineteenth century castle. The poet Yeats was so impressed, both with the castle and the island, that he planned to make it a centre for the study and contemplation of mystical Ireland.

LILY POOL AND TEMPLE
Strokestown Park, Roscommon

Strokestown Park is a splendid eighteenth-century Palladian mansion famous for its collection of original furnishings. In 1997, after a ten-year restoration programme, Strokestown's 2.5-hectare (six-acre) walled gardens were opened to the public for the first time. Among the many original features that have been faithfully restored are this magnificent lily pond and ornamental temple. The gardens appear in the *Guinness Book of Records* for possessing the longest herbaceous border in the whole of the British Isles.

KYLEMORE
Connemara, Galway

Manchester millionaire Mitchell Henry built Kylemore Abbey, a nineteenth-century Gothic Revivalist fantasy on the shores of Fannon Pool, as a gift for his wife after they honeymooned in the area. When his wife and daughter tragically died he sold the property, and in 1916 Kylemore became the Irish home of the Order of Benedictine Nuns, driven from their abbey in Ypres, France by the bombs of the First World War. Today the nuns run a thriving girls school at Kylemore.

COTTAGES
Tullycross, Connemara, Galway

There is an historic, yester-year feel to the landscape of Ireland, and in particular to the relatively isolated and wild area of Galway, a county famed for its small-scale domestic farms. The landscape here is dotted with typical Irish farm cottages, small, often white-washed, sporting colourful front doors and thatched roofs, such as those found in Tullycross village on the Renvyle peninsula. The simple, but aesthetic quality of these small homes perfectly reveals the rural charms of the area.

AUGHRISBEG
near Cleggan, Connemara, Galway

Atlantic gales have lashed the Connemara coast of County Galway for thousands of years. The constant battering of wind and waves has produced a shoreline of beautiful bays, hidden coves and craggy peninsulas that are treacherous for sailors but spectacular when viewed from the safety of the shore. Here in Cleggan Bay, the view west to distant Inishboffin Island is given a poignancy by the silhouette of an anchor beached forlornly on the foreshore.

CONNEMARA PONY
near Cleggan, Galway

In the summer the countryside in Connemara can be rich with wild flowers and green meadows, a very different landscape from the barren moors and desolate bogs of winter. In this challenging natural habitat, the Connemara pony has flourished. Considered Ireland's only native breed, legend has it that they are the result of breeding between local ponies brought to the area by the Celts and Spanish horses swept ashore from the shipwrecked boats of the Spanish Armada.

DOON HILL
Connemara, Galway

Lough Corrib is a vast lake of over 16,000 hectares (40,000 acres), stretching north through Connemara from Galway on the coast into the heart of 'Joyce Country' in the Maumturk Mountains. Famous for its fishing, the lough also has a shoreline that, in places, is as pretty as any in Ireland. The northwestern stretch is particularly highly regarded, and Doon Hill is a popular spot to take in the view. Looking south along the shore is the lonely outline of Aughnanure Castle.

CLIFDEN
Connemara, Galway

In the heart of Connemara, overlooked by the peaks of the Twelve Pins, is the busy little town of Clifden, seen here with the cloud-capped Maumturk Mountain in the distance. Clifden, some 80 km (50 miles) from Galway City, is both the commercial and tourist centre for the region. The two spires that dominate the Clifden skyline are of the neo-Gothic Catholic church, built on the site of a beehive-shaped ancient stone hut, and, nearby, the more austere Protestant church.

SKY ROAD
near Clifden, Galway

Just west of Clifden is the evocatively named Sky Road, an
11 km (7 mile) scenic drive around the Kingstown Peninsula.
Sky Road is actually two roads – one hugs the shoreline while
the other climbs to a height of over 150 m (500 ft). Both
provide spectacular views across to the islands of Inishturk and
Talbot. Here the low road passes a traditional Galway cottage,
with its thatched roof and whitewashed walls nestling into
a heather-covered hillside.

BUNOWEN BAY AND TWELVE PINS
Connemara, Galway

The twelve imposing summits of the Twelve Pins form an
impressive backdrop for the pier harbour at Bunowen Bay.
Wherever you are in Connemara, the Twelve Pins, or Bens
as they are known locally, dominate the view. Benbaun is
the highest peak, rising to 729 m (2,400 ft) while the lowest,
Bengoora, also called Diamond Hill, climbs to 400 m (1,329 ft).
Part of the Maumturk Mountains, this distinctive range of hills
provides excellent hill-walking country with memorable views.

DERRYCLARE LOUGH
Connemara, Galway

The Maumturks, shrouded in cloud, stand between the placid
waters of Derryclare Lough and the sea. This almost mystical
scene can be little changed from the time of the Celts who first
settled on the west coast of Ireland more than 2,500 years ago.
On the western shores of the lough there is a nature reserve of
ancient oak woodland, funded by the Irish American Cultural
Foundation in appreciation of the contribution emigrants from
Galway have made to the life of Boston.

GALWAY CITY
Galway

Walking through its welcoming streets and pleasant squares, you might find it hard to believe that Galway City at the mouth of Lough Corrib is one of the fastest growing urban areas in the European Union. Of all Ireland's cities, Galway is the one that best combines the modern Ireland of the Celtic Tiger with the easy-going vibrancy and cultural richness that is its Gaelic heritage. The gentle harbour with its fishing boats moored to the stone walls give little hint of the activity beyond.

KINVARA
Galway

The likeable little port of Kinvara takes it name from the Irish *cinn mhara*, which translates as 'head of the sea'. Protected by the shelter of Kinvara Bay, Kinvara grew as a gateway for traders from Galway who found the region to be far more accessible by sea than by land. The thriving port's history is celebrated every year at the *Cruinui na mBad*, a festival that sees traditional nineteenth-century Connemara sailing craft competing in hotly contested races across the bay.

DUNGUAIRE CASTLE
Kinvara, Galway

Close to the port at Kinvara, Dunguaire Castle is a small, sixteenth-century fortress marvellously situated on a rocky promontory overlooking the majestic sweep of Galway Bay. In the early twentieth century the castle, built in 1520, became the venue for the meeting of a group of distinguished literary revivalists including W.B. Yeats, his patron Lady Gregory, and the playwrights George Bernard Shaw and J.M. Synge. Today it plays host to somewhat more prosaic twice-nightly medieval banquets.

LEINSTER NORTH

The landlocked counties of Longford, Westmeath and Kildare, and the east coast counties of Louth, Dublin, Meath and Offaly make up what is generally referred to as the Midlands or, more exactly, the Central Lowlands.

Though the region tends to be ignored in favour of its more dramatic and alluring neighbours, Leinster contains some of Ireland's most sacred and culturally important sites. Indeed, these counties are accurately described as the cradle of Irish civilization. As well as lush pastures, rolling hills, lakes and raised peat-land bogs, the Central Lowlands are home to the Republic's capital city Dublin, as well as Tara, the spiritual centre of ancient Ireland and seat of the High Kings of Ireland until the eleventh century.

Monuments of the stature of the Neolithic passage graves of Newgrange dating from 3,000 BC, eleventh-century Mellifont Abbey and the vast Norman fortress at Trim in County Meath, all tell a tale of Ireland just as impressive as the mighty cliffs of Donegal or the otherworldly landscape of County Clare's Burren. The north of Leinster can also offer fine beaches, elegant seaside resorts, and some of the finest horse racing to be found anywhere in the world.

THE PIKEMAN
Ballinamuck, Longford

Of the many rebellions against the English, the 1798 Rebellion was the most widespread. During six months in that year, more than 30,000 Irishmen died as 11 of the 32 counties rose up against the English. The main weapon used by the Irish forces, who were known as the 'United Irishmen', was the pike: a steel or iron spearhead mounted on a wooden shaft. The Pikeman is a memorial to the rebellion, which ended with the rebel force's defeat at Ballinamuck.

EGAN'S BAR
Moate, Westmeath

On the main street of the small village of Moate in Westmeath, Egan's Bar provides a bold splash of colour. Minimal in style, not even displaying the ubiquitous Guinness adverts, the Gaelic-style name ranges boldly across the length of the frontage. The deep red paintwork and the two large plain windows combine to produce an effect that is modern while retaining the feel of a bygone era. Egan's bar has that easy, natural elegance that even professional designers struggle to achieve.

BURIAL CHAMBER AND STANDING STONE
Newgrange, Meath

A summer moon shines over the mysterious burial chamber and standing stone at Newgrange. Celtic tradition suggests that this is the burial place of the legendary kings of Tara, but in fact the chamber predates them by thousands of years. When the tomb was excavated, archaeologists discovered that the light of the winter solstice sun entered the tomb, illuminating the burial chamber. Remarkably, the burial chamber at Newgrange, in this quiet corner of County Meath, is the world's oldest solar observatory.

TRIM CASTLE
Trim, Meath

Trim, now a lively market town in the centre of historic County Meath, was once intended to be Ireland's capital. The most obvious sign of its former glory is the considerable size of Trim Castle, the largest Anglo-Norman castle in Ireland. The massive twenty-sided cruciform tower that forms the three-storied keep was built in around 1200 by Hugh de Lacy, the first Norman baron of Meath. The castle was extensively restored in 2000 as part of Ireland's Millennium Project.

PROLEEK DOLMEN
Cooley Peninsula, Louth

The massive capstone of the Proleek dolmen, or portal tomb, is estimated to weigh more than 30 tons. It has stood balanced precariously on its three supporting stones since 3000 BC when local Neolithic farming communities built it. Just how these primitive farmers managed to construct such a massive and yet delicately balanced structure is still largely unknown. Local folklore predicts that anyone who can throw three stones onto the capstone without any of them falling off will be married within a year.

THE ABBEY AT CLONMACNOISE
Offaly

St Ciaran originally founded the first church on the ancient monastic site at Clonmacnoise in AD 545. Strategically located on the banks of the Shannon at the intersection of a number of important medieval roads, the site supported a religious community that thrived throughout the Middle Ages. Among the remains that survive today are a fifteenth-century cathedral, a fine round tower, many small churches and an important collection of ancient tombstones and thousand-year-old High Crosses.

BIRR CASTLE
Offaly

In the mid-nineteenth century, the 3rd Earl of Rosse, whose family had lived in Birr Castle since its construction in 1620, possessed what was then the largest astronomical telescope in the world, the 'Leviathan'. Birr is equally famous for the splendour of its grounds, which extend to over 60 hectares (150 acres) of parkland and gardens, first laid out in the eighteenth century. Succeeding Earls of Ross have added to the exotic plants and trees on display, often sponsoring foreign expeditions to gather more.

RIVER LIFFEY
Dublin

The River Liffey flows through the heart of Dublin and lends much to the character of this elegant Georgian city. The Vikings established the original settlement in the eighth century naming it from the Irish words *dubh* ('black'), and *linn* ('pool'). It is thought this referred to a black pool in a tributary of the Liffey, which has long since been drained and built over. In the foreground is Ha'penny Bridge, while to the left the dome of the majestic Four Courts building can just be seen.

SCULPTURE OF JIM LARKIN AND THE SPIRE
O'Connell Street, Dublin

In the centre of O'Connell Street, Dublin's principle thoroughfare, stand monuments to Ireland's past and its future. In the foreground, the oversized hands of Big Jim Larkin, the founder of the Irish Transport and General Workers Union in 1909, exhort the workers to rise up against injustice. Behind Jim rises the 120 m (390 ft) high Dublin Spire, the city's tallest structure by some measure. This futuristic stainless steel creation was the winner of a millennium competition to replace the little-loved Nelson's Column, blown up in 1966.

TRINITY COLLEGE
Dublin

Founded by a Royal Charter of Queen Elizabeth I in 1592, Trinity College is one of the world's great seats of learning, and in 1904, it was the first of the ancient universities of the British Isles to admit women. Its manicured lawns and elegant quadrangles have played host to extremely distinguished alumni, including the Nobel Prize-winners Samuel Beckett and Ernest Walton. The 30 m (100 ft) high campanile that confronts visitors as they enter the campus was designed in 1853 by the architect Sir Charles Lanyon.

DUBLIN CASTLE
Dublin

On 16 January 1922, following the signing of the Anglo Irish Treaty, the rebel commander Michael Collins arrived in the Great Courtyard, pictured here, to receive the handover of Dublin Castle. So ended seven long centuries of the castle being one of the most prominent symbols of English rule in Ireland. Following Irish independence, the castle was allowed to fall into disrepair, a decaying symbol of a painful past. Now it is fully restored and integrated into Irish life.

THE DAIL
Government Buildings, Dublin

The Duke of Leinster, who wanted to live in the stateliest mansion in Dublin, originally commissioned Leinster House in 1745. Designed by the German Richard Cassells, it is said to have been a major influence on James Hoban, the Irish architect of the White House in Washington. Since the proclamation of the Irish Free State in 1922, Leinster House has been the seat of the two chambers of the Irish Parliament, Dáil Éireann (the House of Representatives) and Seanad Éireann (the Senate).

CUSTOM HOUSE
River Liffey, Dublin

Of the many notable buildings that the English architect James Gandon designed for Dublin, his crowning achievement was the majestic Custom House on the north bank of the Liffey. Ironically, less than a decade after its completion, the 1800 Act of Union made the building's principal function as the centre for Ireland's customs and excise business redundant. Having fallen into disrepair, and set on fire by Sinn Féin supporters in 1921, it was restored to its former glory in 1991.

HA'PENNY BRIDGE
Dublin

Ha'penny Bridge, an iconic symbol of Dublin, was originally called Wellington Bridge after the 'Iron Duke', Duke of Wellington. Today its formal name is the Liffey Bridge, although it is seldom referred to as anything other than Ha'penny Bridge. Opened in 1816, the bridge was designed and built by John Windsor, the ironwork being produced in Shropshire and shipped to Dublin for assembly. When it was opened there was a toll of half a penny to cross it, and its nickname, Ha'penny Bridge, has stuck.

CHRIST CHURCH CATHEDRAL
Dublin

Dublin has two cathedrals but, unusually for such a Catholic
country, both are part of the Protestant Church of Ireland.
Richard de Clare, Dublin's Anglo Norman conqueror, founded
Christ Church in 1172. It was built on the site of an earlier
Viking church and became a protestant church at the time
of the English Reformation. The cathedral was extensively
remodelled in the late nineteenth century, and the bridge
to Synod Hall, shown here, was built as part of that work.

GEORGIAN DOORS
Dublin

During the eighteenth century, the period known as the Protestant Ascendancy, Anglican landowners dominated Ireland's economic, political and social scene. Not wanting to appear second rate to their counterparts in England, they went to great lengths to demonstrate their wealth and sophistication. Dublin was transformed into one of the most graceful cities in Europe and this fine pair of Georgian doors, flanked by imposing columns and crowned with segmented fanlights, is a legacy of the period.

MALAHIDE CASTLE
Dublin

Malahide Castle, the home of the Talbot family for almost eight centuries, sits in 100 hectares (250 acres) of parkland close to the little seaside town of Malahide not far from Dublin. The castle reflects the Talbot history and has been much altered and added to over the centuries. At its heart is the splendid medieval Oak Room lit by Gothic windows, which are a nineteenth century addition. The castle's hall is one of the finest examples of Norman architecture anywhere in Ireland.

LEINSTER SOUTH

>→◆→O→◆→←

The south of Leinster is the driest and sunniest corner of Ireland, home to ancient monuments, monasteries, fine houses and magnificent gardens.

The gentle seashores of Wicklow and Wexford reflect their sheltered aspect in much the same way as the wild west coast testifies to the insatiable power of the Atlantic. The southeastern coastline is one of dazzling beaches of silver sand, secluded river estuaries, rocky headlands and quiet coastal villages. Further inland, the wild and threatening beauty of the Wicklow Mountains forms a powerful backdrop for the ancient monastic site of Glendalough, and the formal gardens at Powerscourt and Mount Usher. The Wicklow Mountains, once bandit country and home to successive groups of Irish dissidents, are a pointed reminder of Ireland's turbulent past in this comfortable, conservative region.

Beyond the Wicklow Mountains spread green pastures, wooded valleys and swiftly flowing rivers. There are fine towns and pretty villages here too, none more stylish than the inland city of Kilkenny. Reminders of the suffering caused by the great potato famines temper the south of Leinster's easy-going elegance, however. The 'famine walls' that surround many of the great houses of the area were built simply to provide work for the famine's survivors.

PLEACHED LIME ALLEY
Heywood Gardens, Laois

Shakespeare refers to a 'thick pleached allee' in *Much Ado About Nothing*, and an elegant avenue of pleached lime trees was a typical feature of many formal English gardens from the fourteenth century onwards. Completed in 1912, Heywood Gardens in County Laois was the work of two distinguished English designers: the architect Sir Edwin Lutyens and the landscape gardener Gertrude Jekyll. As well as the formal elements, the gardens include lakes, woodlands and architectural features.

STRADBALLY
Laois

The gentle landscape of County Laois, with its lush pastures and neatly laid-out fields, is typical of Ireland's central lowlands. The fertile soil of Laois has attracted settlers from the earliest times. Here and in neighbouring Offaly, the British policy of Plantation was used extensively to secure a base around the Pale, the seat of English authority. This verdant countryside is close to the elegant 'estate town' of Abbeyleix, carefully laid out during the Plantations.

THE CURRAGH RACECOURSE
Kildare

Horse racing may be the sport of kings, but there's no pretentiousness at an Irish race meeting. The Irish love of racing and breeding thoroughbred horses is deeply ingrained and virtually universal. The Curragh, one of the premier flat racing courses in the world, is set in 2,000 hectares (5,000 acres) of rolling Kildare grasslands. The whole area is dotted with stud farms where powerful and aristocratic Irish thoroughbreds, some of the finest racehorses in the world, are bred and exercised.

RED BRIDGE AND JAPANESE LANTERN
Japanese Gardens, Kildare

In 1900, the somewhat eccentric Colonel William Hall Walker, later Lord Wavertree, set up what was to become the National Stud. Walker believed that a racehorse's form could be predicted using astrology, and it has to be said his horses were unusually successful. A further eccentricity of Walker's was the remarkable Japanese garden that he laid out with the help of two Japanese master-gardeners. It traces an allegorical journey through life from the Gate of Oblivion, where life begins, to the Gateway of Eternity.

ST JOSEPH'S SQUARE
St Patrick's College, Maynooth, Kildare

When George III signed the authorization for a Catholic seminary at Maynooth, he remarked that it gave him more pain to do so than losing the American colonies. St Patrick's College, seen here from St Joseph's Square, was founded as the National Seminary for Ireland in 1795, allowing Catholic priests to be educated in Ireland for the first time since the early sixteenth century. Parts of the square are the works of Augustus Pugin, better known as one of the two architects of the Palace of Westminster.

WICKLOW WAY
Wicklow

Commonly referred to as the 'Garden of Ireland', Wicklow is located to the south of Dublin and borders Kildare to the west. It is an extraordinarily beautiful county that is traversed by the picturesque Wicklow Mountains, the longest mountain range in Ireland. Crossing the range, though avoiding the major peaks, is the Wicklow Way, which at 132 km (82 miles), is the longest way-marked trail in Ireland. It was also the first such trail in Ireland, having been formally established in 1980.

BUTTERCUPS STORE
Enniskerry, Wicklow

At some point in the past, the owners of a comfortable house in Main Street, Enniskerry decided to transform part of the downstairs into Buttercups, now a thriving newsagents and general store. Buttercups has all the hallmarks of the small Irish corner shop: brightly coloured paintwork, a profusion of flowers and an unmistakably welcoming ambiance. It would be hard to pass such a shop without popping in for a paper and very possibly an update on the local gossip.

POWERSCOURT GARDENS
Wicklow

A garden of international importance, Powerscourt stands as testimony to the might and wealth of the eighteenth century Anglo-Irish Protestant Ascendancy. Magnificently located in the shadow of the Great and Little Sugarloaf Mountains, everything at Powerscourt is on a grand scale. The formal gardens, sweeping terraces, ornamental lakes and rambling walks cover an area of over 560 immaculately maintained hectares (1,400 acres). Even the drive leading up to the Palladian House is almost 1.65 km (1 mile) long.

MOUNT USHER GARDENS
Wicklow

The important and influential Irish garden designer William
Robinson believed that gardens should be natural rather than
formal: the 'Robinsonian' style is named after him. Laid out
along the banks of the River Vartry in County Wicklow, Mount
Usher Gardens is a perfect example of this style. Begun in 1868
by the Dublin businessman Edward Walpole, the gardens were
extended and developed by his three sons into what is now
one of Ireland finest collection of native and exotic plants.

WICKLOW MOUNTAINS
Wicklow

The Wicklow Mountains are close enough to Dublin to be
easily visible from there, but it would be difficult to imagine two
more contrasting locations. Even the surrounding countryside
gives no hint of the wild and desolate scenery of the mountains.
In the past, the inaccessibility of the terrain made the Wicklow
Mountains bandit country, a lawless area where insurgents could
hide out just a stone's throw from the capital. Today they provide
excellent hiking and climbing terrain.

GLENDALOUGH
Wicklow

The view of the valley of Glendalough and the eleventh
century round tower of St Kevin's monastery are one of
County Wicklow's enduring images. The monastic community
that St Kevin established in the sixth century survived repeated
attacks from the Vikings, flourishing for more than 600 years as
a centre of learning renowned throughout Europe. The 34 m
(112 ft) high round tower itself has survived virtually intact,
only the cap having been restored in the 1870s using the
original stones.

AVOCA
Wicklow

The picturesque village of Avoca set in the Avoca River Valley lies in the heart of County Wicklow mid-way between the towns of Wicklow and Arklow. The great nineteenth-century Irish poet Thomas Moore was famously inspired by the deciduous forests that line the valley, and the Meeting of the Waters where the Avonmore and the Avonbeg rivers meet to form the Avoca River. And if the scene here looks familiar, it's because Avoca was used as the location for the popular BBC television series *Ballykissangel*.

THE THOLSEL AND HIGH STREET
Kilkenny City, Kilkenny

Set in the rich farmlands of the southeast corner of Ireland, Kilkenny City is regarded as Ireland's finest medieval city. The fine eighteenth-century Tholsel with its lantern clock tower and elegant covered arcade was once the centre for tax collecting and a meeting place for merchants. Now Kilkenny's town hall, its unusual name is derived from two old English words: 'toll', meaning tax, and 'sael' meaning hall, hence the place where taxes were paid.

KILKENNY CASTLE
Kilkenny

The splendid medieval form of Kilkenny Castle rises imposingly above Kilkenny City. There has been a castle on this site since 1172 when Richard de Clare, the notorious Strongbow, built the first one. Constructed in 1213, the stone 'keep-less' castle with its massive drum towers forms the heart of what remains today. Although the castle retains its original medieval appearance, much of the structure was rebuilt in the seventeenth and again in the nineteenth centuries.

THE LAKE
Altamont Garden, Carlow

The enchanting contrasts offered by the formal and informal gardens laid out across the 40-hectare (100-acre) estate of Altamont are the result of centuries of planting and nurturing by successive owners. However, as with so much of Ireland, evidence of hardship and the suffering of its people is not far away. The ornamental lake that you see here was dug out by hand after the Irish famine to give employment to local people. It took 100 men two years to complete the work.

MILLFORD MILLS
Carlow

Millford Mills, situated on the east bank of a fast-flowing section of the Barrow River, was established by the Alexander family in the late eighteenth century to grind wheat and was later used as a sawmill. In 1890 the mills were converted into a generating station, and housed Ireland's first hydro-electric power scheme. The electricity generated allowed Carlow to become one of the first towns in the British Isles to experience electric street lighting.

WEXFORD CITY
Wexford

Cosmopolitan Wexford City is a lively place, proud of its varied arts scene and fine selection of pubs and restaurants. Founded by the Vikings and developed by the Normans, Wexford was once a thriving and important port, and its pretty quayside played host to sailing ships from Liverpool and Bristol. Silting of the estuary and harbour in Victorian times stopped this trade, and today only small fishing boats, mussel dredgers and yachts are able to use it.

JOHNSTOWN CASTLE
Wexford

Now an agricultural research centre and home to the Irish Agricultural Museum, Johnstown Castle is an impressive Gothic-Revival Victorian mansion. It was designed by Kilkenny architect Daniel Robertson in 1810 to sit in perfect harmony with the carefully arranged ornamental grounds which are the estate's real glory. The grand five-acre lake in front of the house is not a natural feature, but was dug at the same time as a lower lake and a splendid sunken Italian Garden.

KILMORE QUAY
Wexford

Kilmore Quay is a delightfully unspoilt little village of thatched cottages with whitewashed walls gathered around a stonewall harbour. Moored in the harbour, the perfectly preserved 1923 lightship *The Guillemot* is home to the Kilmore Maritime Museum. From the quay, boat trips leave for the nearby Saltee Islands, where there are puffins, gannets and large colonies of cormorants. The area is noted for the quality of the lobster and deep-sea fishing, and the village holds a hugely popular Sea Festival in July.

BOOLEY BAY
Hook Peninsula,
Wexford

On the tapering headland of the Hook Peninsula, the sun sets dramatically on the ebbing tide at Booley Bay. Booley shelters in the estuary of the River Barrow, an area of 'lost' villages overcome by tidal silting and floodwaters driven by tides and strong winds running up the coast. Just inland from the shifting sands of the bay is Duncannon, where in 1690 James II finally fled Ireland after his disastrous defeat at Battle of the Boyne.

HOOK HEAD
Wexford

Lighthouses are by their nature remarkable buildings, and few are more astounding than the lighthouse at Hook Head. There may have been a lighthouse on this site earlier, but we know for sure that in 1172 the Norman Raymond le Gros built the existing structure with its 4 m (13 ft) thick walls. Originally manned by monks, the lighthouse's peat-fire beacon was guiding sailors into the safety of the Waterford Estuary more than six centuries before the pioneering eighteenth-century British lighthouses of James Smeaton.

MUNSTER NORTH

Even in a country so blessed with stunning scenery, Munster is special. The counties of the north of Munster are united by Ireland's longest river, the majestic Shannon, which flows through all three of them on the final stages of its journey to the Atlantic. However, the coastal scenery and relative emptiness of County Clare contrast with the more populous and fertile counties of Limerick and Tipperary.

Among its many treasures, County Clare has two defining geological features. In the north of the county lies the austere landscape of the Burren. This vast desolate limestone plateau shows little sign of life other than the truly remarkable diversity of Alpine and Mediterranean flowers and plants that reappear every summer. Further south, facing out to the Aran Islands and the ocean's gales are the Cliffs of Moher. Their vertiginous sheer rock faces, home to legions of seabirds, form one of the most dramatic outlooks of Ireland's breathtaking west coast.

Limerick and Tipperary cannot compete with the drama of the Clare coast, but both counties have more than their share of pleasant towns, country estates, ruined castles, abbeys and ancient monuments, all set in gentle, rolling landscapes.

POULNABRONE DOLMEN
The Burren, Clare

In the heart of the stark landscape of the Burren stands the magnificent Poulnabrone dolmen. Poulnabrone, a wedge tomb, is the finest of over 70 ancient burial sites to be found in the Burren's limestone uplands and consists of four upright stones supporting a thin capstone. When the tomb was excavated in the 1960s, the remains of 20 adults, five children and a newborn baby were uncovered. Subsequent carbon dating calculated the burials took place between 3800 and 3200 BC.

BALLYVAUGHAN
near the Burren, Clare

The pretty fishing village of Ballyvaughan looks north across Galway Bay from its location on the edge of the Burren. Although the village only developed as a fishing community in the nineteenth century, the ruins of a Celtic ring fort and castle suggest that this sheltered bay was inhabited much earlier. In the summer Ballyvaughan is a glorious spot full of charming cottages with neat gardens that give little indication of the Atlantic gales that batter them in the winter months.

CLIFFS OF MOHER
Clare

Although not as high as the cliffs at Slieve League in County
Donegal, the Cliffs of Moher are every bit as dramatic. Rising
vertically to a height of 200 m (650 ft) out of the crashing waves
of the Atlantic, their sheer rock faces extend for over 8 km
(5 miles) along the coast of County Clare. In any light, the
contrasting layers of sandstone and shale of which the cliffs are
composed make a breathtaking sight as the sun sets into the ocean.

NELLY'S PUB
near the Cliffs of Moher, Clare

For the visitor to the windswept magnificence of the Cliffs
of Moher, Nelly's pub can be a welcome source of refuge.
Standing on its own, just back from the cliff face, it provides
a splash of colour with its rich salmon pink walls, and portrait
of (we assume) Nelly herself looking on. The attractive red
hay-cart casually left in the corner of the car park, and the
milk churns, hint at an earlier, more rural clientele.

SPANISH POINT
Clare

In 1558 Philip II of Spain assembled an Armada of 131 ships to attack the English forces of the Protestant Queen Elizabeth I. The ill-fated fleet was forced to flee, returning to their base in the Mediterranean via the west coast of Ireland. A hurricane drove many of the ships ashore on the reefs around Spanish Point, where 5,000 Spanish sailors perished either at sea or at the hands of the English authorities when they landed.

BUNRATTY CASTLE
near Shannon, Clare

Now one of Ireland's most popular tourist attractions, the formidable Bunratty Castle stands four-square against the evening sky. The last in a series of fortified structures built to exploit the strategic site, the castle was built in the fifteenth century. The exterior remains faithful to the original design and the magnificently restored interior is much as it was in the mid-seventeenth century. In the grounds of the castle is a detailed recreation of Irish rural life – Bunratty Folk Park.

KING JOHN'S CASTLE
AND RIVER SHANNON
Limerick

The King's Island in the heart of Limerick City is formed by
a loop of the River Shannon and is connected to the mainland
city by four bridges. Mighty King John's Castle stands by the
Thomond Bridge, guarding the river and the city. Its five
massive drum towers and its solid curtain walls were built
to withstand the primitive but awesome power of thirteenth-
century siege machines. Even today, eight centuries after the
castle was built, it is an imposing sight.

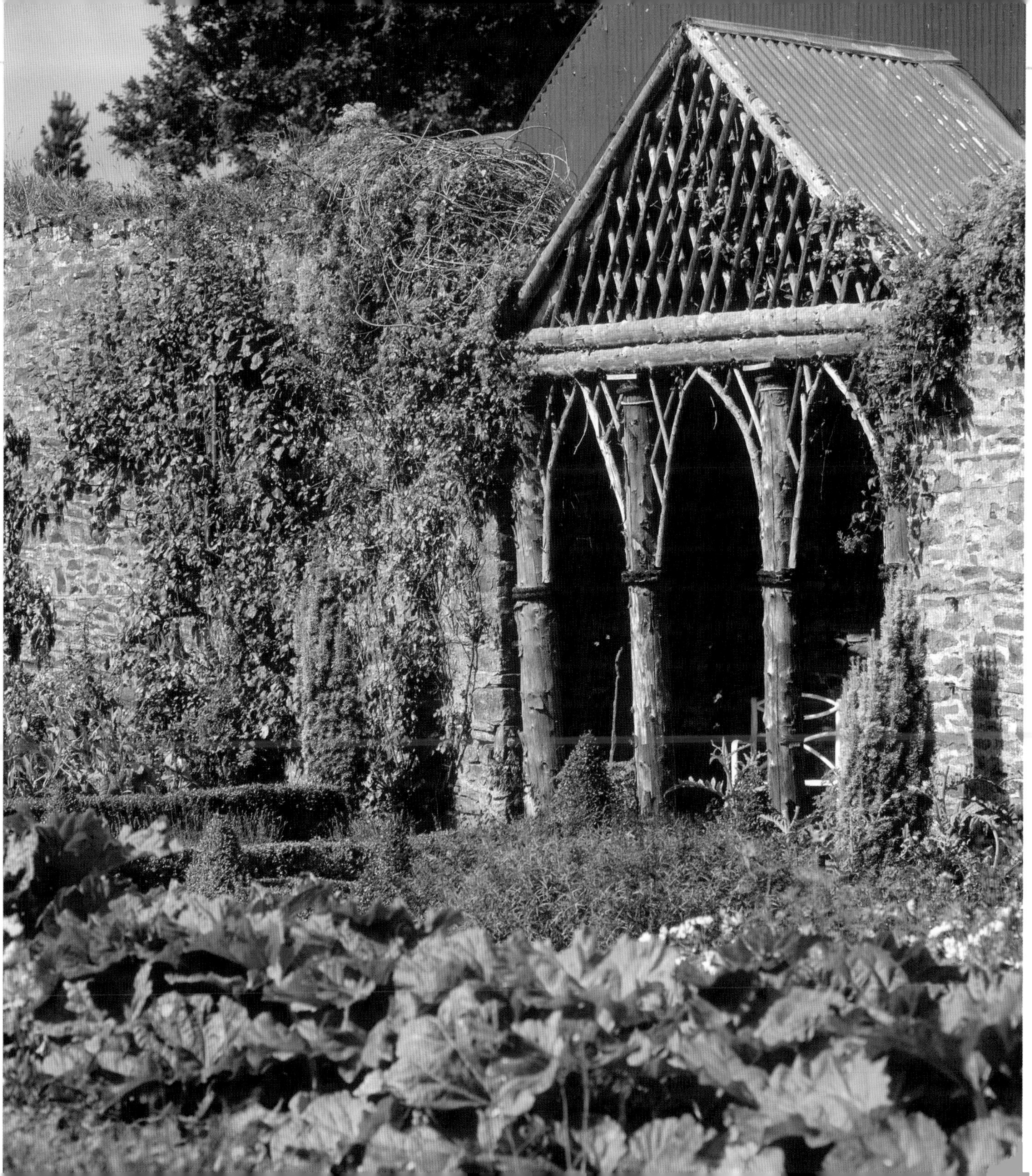

RUSTIC TEMPLE
Walled Garden, Glin Castle, Limerick

Glin Castle is not so much a castle as a rather splendid Georgian House with castellations added later. A feature of the house is its unusually large number of windows, 'one for every day of the year', the locals suggest. The 200-hectare (500-acre) estate on the banks of the Shannon includes fine formal gardens and extensive fruit and vegetable kitchen gardens. There is also a restored Victorian 'lost' garden complete with Gothic hermitage and this rather lovely rustic temple with echoes of the Gothic style.

ADARE
Limerick

Situated on the Maigue, a tributary of the Shannon, Adare takes it name from the Gaelic *Ath Dara*, the 'ford of the oak'. The old town of Adare, in the shadow of Desmond Castle, was destroyed during the wars of the sixteenth century. The present village, with its irresistibly picturesque thatched and whitewashed cottages, dates back to the nineteenth century when the Earl of Dunraven laid out the streets and built the dwellings according to his own design.

ROCK OF CASHEL
Tipperary

Rising up on a limestone outcrop beside the Dublin to Cork road is the great stone fort of Cashel, with its 28 m (93 ft) high round tower scanning the horizon for potential attacks. From the fourth century Cashel was the seat of the Kings of Munster and Brian Boru was crowned here in 977. In 1100 Cashel was handed over to the church and a religious community flourished here until 1647 when Cromwell's army laid siege to it, finally massacring its 3,000 inhabitants.

CAHIR CASTLE
Tipperary

The busy market town of Cahir on the River Suir was once an important garrison town. Its castle, built on a rocky island in the middle of the river, is one of the most redoubtable of Ireland's many well-fortified bastions. Built in the thirteenth century, the castle was the domain of the powerful Anglo-Norman Butler family from 1375 until 1964. The Butlers maintained their castle well, renovating and extending it periodically through the centuries so that today it remains remarkably well preserved.

THE SWISS COTTAGE
near *Cahir, Tipperary*

The enchanting Swiss Cottage provides a wonderful antidote to
formidable Cahir Castle. In 1810 the Butlers commissioned John
Nash, the English Regency architect, to produce a rustic folly
in the grounds of their castle. Nash's design for Swiss Cottage,
a cottage orné, fulfils all the elaborate conditions of that genre,
where all the features of the design are drawn from nature and
nothing matches. Every window, door, archway, roofline and eve
of the cottage is of differing dimensions and design.

MUNSTER SOUTH

>─┼─◆>──◆─O──◆─<┼─<

The three counties that form the south of Munster track the coastline's transformation from the storm-tossed ruggedness of the west coast to the relative tranquillity and sweeping bays of the south and southeast.

Wild and mountainous County Kerry, still referred to as 'the Kingdom' because of its history of fierce independence from central government, has some of Ireland's finest scenery – its greatest pre-historic and early Christian monuments and some of its best beaches. Killarney National Park, with its romantic lakes and mountains, has been a fashionable tourist destination since Victorian times, and the Dingle Peninsula's combination of enchanting scenery and important historic sites makes it an outstanding area of international renown.

County Cork's slightly more sheltered southerly aspect has produced a shoreline of impressive bays and magnificent headlands, gentle harbours and long, golden strands. Inland, Cork is a county of rich farmland and pleasant rural backwaters. It is also home to Blarney Castle, resting place of the Blarney Stone, that legendary source of the nation's eloquence. Waterford City, founded by Vikings in the ninth century, is Ireland's oldest city, and a thriving European port. The countryside of County Waterford, though less dramatic than its two larger neighbours, is no less beautiful.

BOG VILLAGE
Ring of Kerry, Kerry

Peat lands, more usually referred to as bogs, cover more than 15 per cent of Ireland and are some of the largest areas of peat in Europe. These large areas of decayed vegetation, laid down over many centuries, were once even more common in Ireland, but a thousand years of cutting peat to use as domestic fuel has left them seriously and irrevocably depleted. The Kerry Bog Village is a meticulous recreation of what a village in the west of Ireland would have looked like at the turn of the nineteenth century.

ANNASCAUL
The Dingle Peninsula, Kerry

The village of Annascaul is situated in the southern foothills of the Slieve Mish Mountains that form the backbone of the Dingle Peninsula. The local beach, Inch Strand, was the location for David Lean's film *Ryan's Daughter*. Annascaul's own claim to fame is Dan Foley's pub and more particularly its brilliantly colourful frontage, which the late, and somewhat eccentric, Dan painted himself some years ago. Foley's is said to be the most photographed pub in Ireland.

SLEA HEAD
The Dingle Peninsula, Kerry

Looking west from Slea Head, across Coumeenoole Bay, lies Dunmore Head, mainland Ireland's most westerly point. Beyond the Head, across Blasket Sound, are the Blasket Islands. Uninhabited since 1953, but once the home of a close-knit community of farmers and fishermen who eked out a living, this inhospitable but beautiful spot is 3.2 km (two miles) off the coast. There are two internationally celebrated accounts of life on the Blasket Islands written by past inhabitants: Maurice O'Sullivan's *Twenty Years A-Growing*, and *Peig* by Peig Sayer.

THE SKELLIGS FROM VALENTIA ISLAND
Kerry

The popular resort of Valentia Island, from where the first transatlantic cable was laid in 1866, is joined to the Dingle Peninsula by a modern causeway that spans the 120 m (400 ft) wide channel. On the horizon, Great and Little Skellig rise precipitously out of the ocean. On Great Skellig, also known as Skellig Michael, is a small ruined sixth-century monastery perched on a ledge almost 220 m (725 ft) above sea level. Today both islands are the exclusive preserve of sea birds that breed there in huge numbers.

ST FINIAN'S BAY AND PUFFIN ISLAND
Kerry

St Finian's Bay, just south of Valentia Island, has one of the Iveragh Peninsula's most spectacular beaches with magnificent views out to the Skelligs. The beach is unsafe for bathing but the presence of the Skellig Chocolate Factory is some consolation. Close to the bay, just 250 m (820 ft) across Puffin Sound, is Puffin Island. This small uninhabited island, an important nature reserve administered by BirdWatch Ireland, is home to large populations of Atlantic puffins, European storm-petrels and Manx sheerwaters.

WATERVILLE
Ring of Kerry, Kerry

Situated on the narrow isthmus between Ballinskelligs Bay
and Lough Currane, Waterville is one of the more sophisticated
resorts on the Kerry coast. Its stony beach and wild views of the
ocean made it popular with Victorians and Edwardians wanting
to get away from the excesses of the more popular resorts
further around the coast. Today it maintains its rather limpid
air of nineteenth century elegance and is famous for having
been Charlie Chaplin's regular choice for family holidays.

LOUGH CURRANE
Waterville, Kerry

A narrow isthmus is all that divides Lough Currane from the
sea in Ballinskelligs Bay. This tranquil spot on the Ring of Kerry,
in the foothills of the Coomcalee Mountains, has a number of
interesting historic ruins including the sixth century Oratory of
St Finan, a twelfth century Hiberno-Romanesque church, and
a partially submerged castle. What brings most people to Lough
Currane is its fish, however, and the lough is acknowledged as
one of the greatest game-fishing locations in Europe.

DERRYNANE BAY
Deenish & Scariff Islands, Kerry

As well as having some of the most spectacular scenery in
the world, Kerry's west-facing coast enjoys some wonderfully
memorable sunsets. Here, looking west from Lamb's Head on
the southern tip of Derrynane Bay, the sun sets over the small
islands of Deenish and Scariff. The bay, with its well-hidden
natural harbour, was a spot much favoured by smugglers. Daniel
O'Connell, the 'Liberator', who won the vote for Irish Catholics
in the nineteenth century, lived at nearby Derrynane house.

WEST COVE
Kerry Peninsula, Kerry

Nestling in the shelter of the north coast of the Kenmare Estuary is West Cove. Its deep-water harbour and sheltered aspect has made it popular with yachtsmen and boating enthusiasts, who relish the fine sailing around the Iveragh Peninsula and south to Bantry Bay and Mizen Head. The views from West Cove harbour south across the river estuary to the mountains of the Slieve Miskish Mountains of the Beara Peninsula are particularly fine.

MOLL'S GAP
Ring of Kerry, Kerry

The Ring of Kerry, a 175-kilometre (110-mile) circuit of the Iveragh Peninsula, is surely one of the best-known tourist routes anywhere in the world. From the gentle grace of Killarney on Lough Leane, through the wild mountain landscape of Macgillycuddy's Reeks to the rugged Kerry coastline, every mile of the journey is filled unforgettable vistas. Moll's Gap, situated in the heart of the mountainous landscapes of the Reeks, is the highest point on the route, looking out over Gap of Dunloe and the Kenmare river.

RING OF KERRY
CARAVAN & CAMPING
PARK

km
13

Páirc Náisiúnta
Chill Áirne
KILLARNEY
NATIONAL PARK

km
7

THE BLUE BULL
RESTAURANT

RIVERSDALE HOUSE
HOTEL &
RESTAURANT

6

Km
10
HILLCREST
FARMHOUSE
Bed & Breakfast

LAKE

km An Óige
8 HOSTEL

SNEEM
Ring of Kerry, Kerry

Midway between Kenmare and Waterville, Sneem is a pleasant riverside town at the head of the Sneem, a tributary of the Kenmare. Like many of the towns and villages on the Ring of Kerry, Sneem has re-invented itself as a tourist destination, naming itself the 'Knot in the Ring', *sneem* being the Gaelic for 'knot'. Its principle hotel, the Parknasilla, lays claim to the unusual distinction of having hosted George Bernard Shaw, President De Gaulle of France and the Queen of the Netherlands.

KILLARNEY NATIONAL PARK
Kerry

At the foot of the Macgillycuddy's Reeks mountain range lie the Lakes of Killarney, surrounded by woodland, rivers and dramatic waterfalls. This area is known as Killarney National Park, the first national park to be set up in Ireland, created when Muckross Estate was donated to the nation in 1932. Today the park encompasses an area of over 10,236 hectare (26,000 acres) of diverse ecology and is home to Ireland's only native herd of red deer.

TORC WATERFALL
Ring of Kerry, Kerry

A much-photographed feature and popular stopping point on the Ring of Kerry is the Torc Waterfall that tumbles into Muckross Lake, one of the three lakes in the Killarney National Park. The 18 m (60 ft) high waterfall marks the mouth of the Owengariff River as it ends its journey from the Torc Mountains through the woods of Friar's Glen. A pretty path winds up to a viewing platform at the top of the falls from where there are splendid views of the mountains.

175

MUCKROSS HOUSE
Killarney, Kerry

Elegant Muckross House overlooks the three lakes in the heart of the Killarney National Park. Designed by the Scottish architect William Burn, the house was built in the 1830s for Henry Herbert and his wife Mary, a noted watercolourist. Successive generations of Herberts had lived at Muckross for over two centuries and the present mansion was the fourth house constructed for them on this lovely site. The splendid gardens were originally laid out for a visit Queen Victoria made in 1861.

ROSS CASTLE
Killarney, Kerry

The setting for Ross Castle on the shores of Killarney's Lower Lake has a fairytale quality that belies its violent history. The ruined tower house is all that remains of the castle that was originally built in the late fifteenth century as the principal seat of the O'Donaghues, ancient kings of Munster. In 1652 the castle was valiantly held against Cromwell's massively superior force of 1,500 infantry and 700 cavalry, only finally succumbing when floating batteries bombarded it from the waters of the lough.

ALLIHIES
Beara Peninsula, Cork

Lying between the southern shore of the Kenmare River and Bantry Bay, the Beara Peninsula marks the start of the transition from wild County Kerry to the increasingly more gentle coastal landscapes of County Cork. The peninsula itself is dominated by the Slieve Miskish and Caha Mountains that run down its spine. Allihies on the more exposed northern coast in Ballydonegan Bay is famous for the ruined Berehaven copper mine, which had an operational depth of over 450 m (1,485 ft).

BANTRY HOUSE
Cork

The White family, formerly the Earls of Bantry, have lived in Bantry House since the seventeenth century when they purchased it as a small Queen Anne house known as Blackrock. It was substantially enlarged in the 1820s by the first Earl of Bantry and subsequently by his son, who furnished it with the famously eclectic collection of furniture that survives to this day. Bantry House has a genuinely magnificent location overlooking the waters of Bantry Bay and the Caha Mountains beyond.

GARINISH ISLAND
Cork

The southwest corner of Ireland, particularly west Cork, is blessed with the warming currents of the Gulf Stream, resulting in relatively mild springs and autumns. The 15-hectare (38-acre) island garden of Garinish, situated in the sheltered waters of the Glengarriff Estuary in Bantry Bay, takes full advantage of the temperate climate. Known to horticulturists worldwide, this remarkable collection of exotic plants and shrubs was first laid out in 1910 by the owner Annan Bryce and the architect and garden designer Harold Peto.

GLANDORE
Cork

Overlooking its tiny stonewalled harbour, Glandore village
is little more than one street of houses hugging the bay in
a wooded south-facing valley. Although only a small village,
Glandore was one of the earliest settlements in West Cork,
and today its sheltered aspect, and its position in the path
of the Gulf Stream, has made it extremely popular with the
sailing community. Above the village are two castles built
by the Normans in the eleventh century and continuously
inhabited up to the present day.

DROMBEG STONE CIRCLE
Cork

The Bronze Age stone circle at Drombeg, not far from Skibbereen, is an important ancient site. Situated on a gentle hillside, the circle has a diameter of about 9 m (30 ft). Thirteen of the original seventeen stones that made up the circle still survive, its two 1.8 m (6 ft) high portal stones located on its northeast side. Facing the entrance formed by the portal stones is a flat altar stone, on which the rays of the setting sun fall at the winter solstice.

BLARNEY CASTLE
Cork

Blarney Castle, built in 1446 by Dermot McCarthy, King of Munster, is one of Ireland's oldest and most historic fortresses. The castle was the third to be built on the site by the McCarthys, whose stronghold it remained until Cromwell finally took it in the seventeenth century. Impressive as the castle is, it is the presence of the Blarney Stone, now rather prosaically referred to as the Stone of Eloquence, which makes Blarney Castle so internationally famous.

RED STRAND AND GALLEY HEAD
Cork

The sandy beaches of West Cork's southern coast are famous for their safe bathing and the natural beauty of their locations. Red Strand is a glorious stretch of golden sand that forms a bay between the two headlands of Galley Head and Dunowen Head. The beach itself is not actually red, its name coming from the colour of the cliffs that shelter it. The area around is particularly noted for its birdlife, and the presence of the wrecks of numerous ships also make it popular with divers.

COBH CATHEDRAL
Cork

Known by the Anglo Irish name of Queenstown for many years, Cobh reverted to its Irish name in 1922 with the founding of the Irish Free State. A pleasant town situated on Great Island in Cork's extensive harbour, Cobh was the embarkation point for hundreds of thousands of Irish men and women forced to leave their homeland by famine and persecution. Cobh's Catholic Cathedral, designed by the celebrated English architects Pugin and Ashlin, is a fine example of the neo-Gothic style.

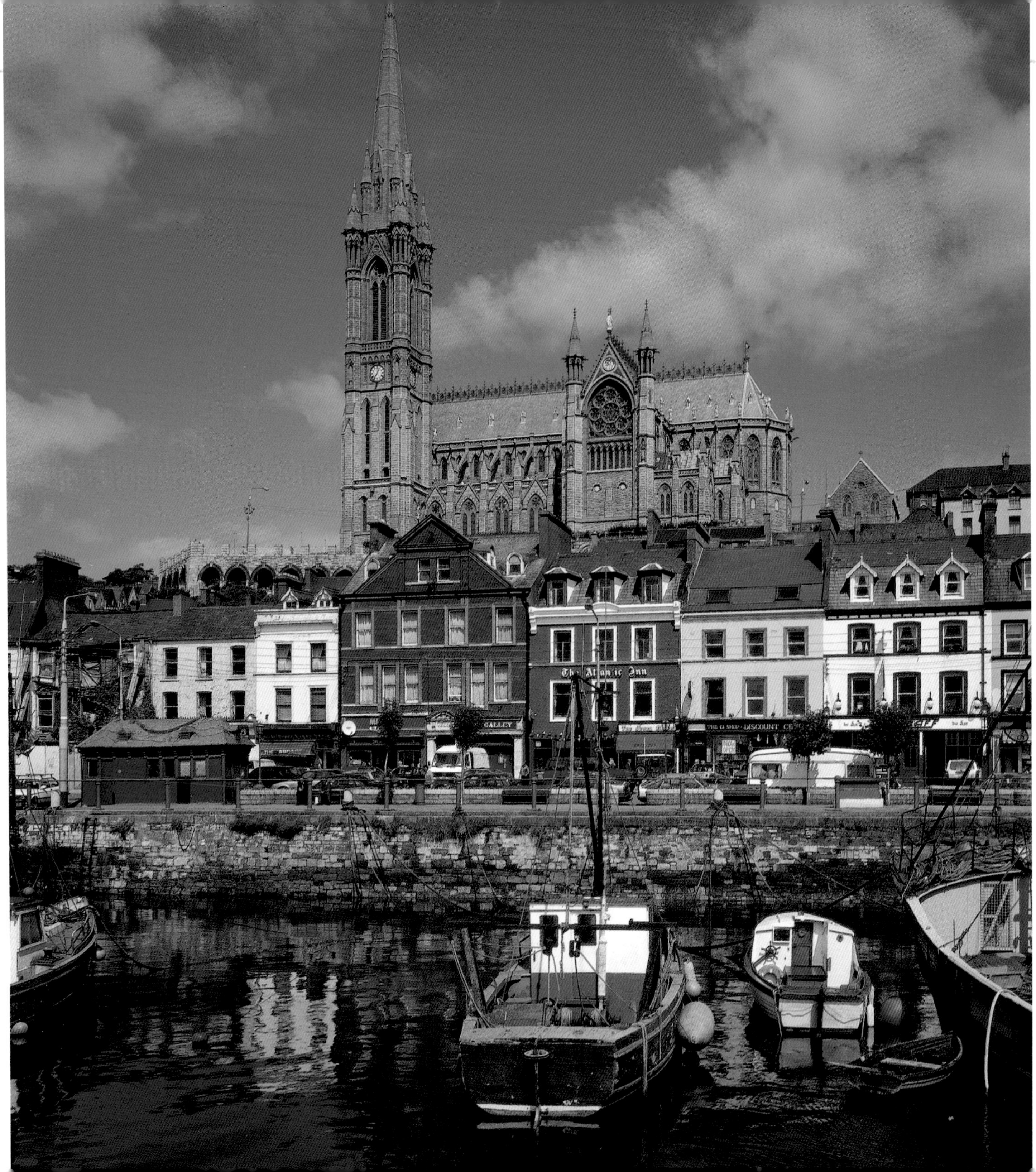
The Atlantic Inn

LISMORE CASTLE
Waterford

Lismore has been the home of the Dukes of Devonshire since the marriage of the fourth Duke to Lady Charlotte Boyle (a descendant of Robert Boyle, the father of modern chemistry) in 1753. It is a marvellously preserved structure, parts of which date back to the thirteenth century. The castle has had more than its share of illustrious residents, having been the property of Sir Walter Raleigh, the Boyle family and the home for the first part of his life of Joseph Paxton, designer of the Crystal Palace in London.

DUNGARVAN
near Waterford, Waterford

Dungarvan, a charming seaside town, is part of what now describes itself as the Irish Riviera, an area of the south coast that spreads east from Cobh in County Cork to Dungarvan itself, and includes the resorts of Ballycotton, Youghal and Ardmore. The town is grandly positioned beneath the Drum Hills at the head of the bay that forms Dungarvan Harbour. It combines the roles of market town, port and tourist resort with an easy-going energy.

INDEX

>─┼─◆─◆─┼─◄